UDAARI

www.writingsofvinati.com

ISBN: 1977627331
ISBN-13: 978-1977627339

for my thirteen year old self.
thank you for picking up a pen and paper that night.

"I know you're tired but come, this is the way."

— Jalaluddin Rumi

beneath the crust
of fallen
leaves

a new season awaits.

_____

beginnings.

let morning hues
be a gentle reminder

of how much more
there is left
to love.

that little warmth
kindling
in your heart

that is where
all the good things reside.

———————

know where to look darling.

it will hurt yes.
you will bleed profusely yes.

but keep plucking out
the noise
which was forcefully fed
to your throat

until what remains of you is you.
only you.
bare. raw. pure.

_____

remainder.

i am
a soft mellow thing.
it is hard not to turn brittle

every time
you
lay your eyes on me.

v i n a t i

embrace your
flaws
like the earth
embraces the rain.

softly
with love.

0

you are allowed to feel
this deeply.

not everyone can fathom
the depths you
carry.

the night kept the moon
for itself.

so i started building
my own.

_____

artwork.

if it doesn't flutter under your flesh
if it doesn't break into you
and swell

in your blood
it is not your passion.

you don't learn to
unlove them.

you learn
to
love yourself more.

_____

how time heals.

the dawn breaks
and you escape into me
spreading like a story
a flame

a riot within
the fine lines of my body.

something
that flows through the limbs
and doesn't know
how to stop.

deep within
the hollow of my chest
these poems rest like
summer.

come
let me keep you warm.

———————

summer vibes.

to fall off my lips
and stay stuck in my words.

that is
what you do best.

follow me to the
stars
and i will show you

how to burn
without
reducing into ash.

it is only when you
stop looking
you find a reason
to
smile.

you smell a lot like
the ocean.

maybe this is why
you keep coming back
in waves.

within the quiet space
of
your ribs

you hold
an entire universe.

_____

there.

that is the thing about
people
who are more soul
than flesh.

you drown in them
and
still do not sink.

we wear each other
like
winter stains.
always close
and always cold.

some days
your thought splits
my spine in
half

and i don't collapse.

_____

good days.

the sun sits
safely
tucked in your pores
and here you are

worrying
about the color of your
skin.

———————

brown.

one day i will brush off
the splintered pieces
of
storm

that was once
my whole life and gradually
crawl away.
uncovered

unguarded
but not vulnerable.
because fighting fear is the most
beautiful
yet terrifying way to know

that you are strong
and
that you always have been.

i'll keep you in the midst
of my ache.

when they fall for my
softness
i will tell them it is you.

_____

maa.

pull yourself
out
of your flesh.
burn down those walls.
uncover your bones

and see
how fiercely you bloom
when you let your body
breathe.

———————

raw.

we were meant to be silent.
my words
spoke to me one day.

like sand
seeping through fingers
and watching it with
broken sighs.

we were meant to be silent
like unfinished
goodbyes.

hold on to your
madness.

this battle
is not beautiful.

sometimes
when the world sleeps

i sit back
and watch myself
crumble
into the midnight calm.

———————

quietude.

you could shred into
shards
and
still heal.

not all warriors
wear metal armors
and
carry swords.

some wear only a
smile.

i've been holding you
in heavy sighs

and i don't know if it is
a good thing.
but there is so much

more
to this weight that keeps me
together. keeps me warm

like summer

strolling in
late

but at last.

we are both made of
infinities

plastered carefully
with skin.

a thousand sunsets melted
in you

when you peeled off the
layers of comfort
from your limbs.

do that often.
you look good

when you wear your soul
inside out.

_____

naked.

today i unearth
the seasons collapsing
in my ribs
flowing graciously

along the lines that turn brown
under the sun.

today i carry myself
quietly
through
the rubble of unspoken words.

today i remind my worth
to this
weak ailing heart.

today i unapologetically choose me.

how is your day going love?

————

the things i speak in hushed tones in
the middle of the day.

the moon slid
within the creases of the night

while you
were collecting dreams.

———————

folds.

my skin smells of poetry.
tell me
how am i not art?

you were not born with a voice
to bury it whenever
they
tell you to.

perhaps
the problem is

we are all
living
a beautiful story

but are completely unaware.

it will take time
to
unstitch

your name
from my tongue

which is still thick
with love.

pause the world and heal.

don't pull out
your soul
for every person

who breathes
summer

into your mouth

because sometimes the light
is too bright

and the heat is too much.

i like the way you
walk into me.

quietly

like
you have always
lived here.

_____

home.

if you must break
don't hold yourself back.

there is nothing more
tragic
than tying the pieces

that don't fit.

i am not the leaf that
falls off you
in the light wind.

i am the soil that holds you.

keeps you strong
in the storm.

you cannot grow
without
growing into me.

_____

root.

somewhere in between
i found prayers

that had fallen
from my mother's lips

when the nights were quiet
the sleep was
deep

and the world was
mine.

———————

how magic happens.

keep dancing
in the wild wind.

the dust will settle
at
its own pace.

but darling
you are a river.

the rocks will
break you.
the valleys will bend you.

but you will never
stop

because
that is what you do.
you flow.

if you let me
i will build a path
of words
to reach your insides

and mute the voices
eating you.

the night breathes
softly

through my eyes
and you ask me

why darkness
feels

familiar to you.

some people leave like this.
their fire condenses

and trickles down.
a cold soot in your bones.

and you live
choking on things

that do not know how to stay.
_____

transience.

listen to the i in me.
it breathes too.

i'm not sure
what pulls me towards
you.

your weak
twisted
heart

or the fact
that it still beats.

you don't teach
an ocean
how to carry its
vastness.
you don't teach a human too.

_____

things we learn ourselves.

it is okay to be
a shadow

before you be the sun.

fall in love with a poet
and
she will weave you.
your smell. the glint in your

eyes. the freckle on
your nose.
the birthmark on your temple.
the soft sighs. the stifled cries.

that stubborn voice. those
childlike laughs.

whole of you.

she will weave
stitch and carve
into a stunning piece of art.

fall in love with a poet darling
and
you will

lose your breath
a thousand times over

contd.

only to find it in her words
again.
again.

and again.

we are everything we seek
yet we wait
patiently

for our ordinary stars
to shine in

an extraordinary
manner.

i am a spark.
wild enough to light up
your
madness.

every time you shame
your body
for wearing too much
or too little earth

a continent weeps.

———————

be black. be brown. be white. be you.

soaked in poetry
dripping
in metaphors

how can i not
reek
of love?

———————

sillage.

be a wildflower.
grow
wherever
your heart beats.

you have so many
lives to live.

it is cruel
to let one of them
spill
a lifetime of chaos in you.

i knew you would
tear me apart.
but i also knew

i would
not
break.

———————

mama fed me resilience.

they cannot water down
your flames

with hands too cold
to feel the heat.

be patient with your soul.
it growls
when it is damaged.

it is not easy
to fold oneself in darkness

and not fall for
the moon.

i have seen you fail
every night.

v i n a t i

before the sky
sinks
into your lap
break open yourself darling.

you cannot heal
without letting the sun in.

do not
build verses

with words
which are not meant for you.

it is in the seething flames
i miss you the most.

the way they bend
towards me

like
i bend
towards you.

_____

trajectory.

fall in love with yourself.
s l o w l y
one
breath
at a time.

all it takes
is a
soft thunder

to traverse the darkest
night.

you are chaos.
a storm.
a story undone.

you are too lush for eyes
that cannot
look into the sun.

sometimes
the most courageous thing
to do

is to believe still.

in people
and in yourself.

i was not born with roses
in my chest
to be afraid of thorns.

i was born to
bloom
in spite of them.

vinati

the earth shudders
and the deepest ocean
moans.

the kind of love they would
not
tell you about.

————————

the kind that rebels.

74

some poems

sit in my stomach
and starve.

this is what your absence
does.

this is what
your presence does
too.

know
that you have been
touched by fire

if my thought
keeps you warm

against the cold
of
your skin.

maybe one day
we will outgrow the maze
of what ifs

and start a story
we want to know the end of.

v i n a t i

the world
is a broken mess
but give it a chance.

let it heal you
with
all its pieces.

because it will.
it always does.

it always
will.

will.

you are not trivial.
there are sorrows rising and falling

in you
like the sea

yet here you are
stealing
another breath for the heart.

i cannot tell
what lures me more.

the september moon
waiting

for winter

or your eyes
waiting for me.

don't beat light out of your
heart.
its darkness
is just as beautiful.

———————

contrast.

there are people who leave
craters behind
in our chest.
in our soul. in our spine.

seek them
and worship them

for they are the ones
who teach us

how to build a garden
out of
nothingness.

losing ourselves
in the chaos is like

losing the little spark
of fire
that we have

and there is nothing
worse

than extinguishing
the only thing
that could light us into a star.

i am too full of
the sun
to be mournful of the rain.

we don't differ in appearance
says dusk to dawn.

we differ in the aftermath
of when we are gone.

i know there are horrors
residing in you

growing on you

eating your insides
making you
weak
frail and fragile.

i know you are
putting on another mask

another layer
of skin to silence them
to shut them out.

but remember love
nothing

in this entire world
is more beautiful

and
more brave

contd.

than blooming
out of
the ugliest

realities
that you survive.

that we survive.

_____

another mask.

one of these days
i will sprout
without the sun

and grow a forest
in the dark.

you have kept
your soul
tied down for too long.

how many more wars
would you eat

to open
yourself to light?

i am in awe
of how we wither
for someone

who is meant to keep us
whole.

winds change.
so do you.
so does the world.

there is nothing more human than this.

in the quietest way
we sew ourselves into

one another
and still breathe apart.

it does not have to
make sense to make you
happy.

_____

a thing to remember. a thing to keep
in the middle of your heart. safe.
warm. and tight.

some days i'm a shipwreck
and i smile.

i think it is you.

smeared
down
to my bones.

someone
who threw me apart
only to keep me off the coast.

_____

debris.

soak your scars
in
the soft sea.

let it teach you how to rise
up to the moon.

do not panic
if
you look for me
in every word

and forget
the language you
breathe.

in a world
that never fails to bring down
the wild and free

it takes courage
to be
a ridiculous dreamer.

i'm not
afraid
to shed the old skin

that smells of
you.

i'm afraid
to uncover what lies
underneath.

a quiet tremble
and we moan

like
the sky
dipped in december nights.

you have a space
here.
don't shrink.
don't contract.

the world will learn
to align itself
with
galaxies burning in you.

a waning moon is
still a moon

even when the wolves don't howl.

to unchain the mind
from

the clutches
of people is a war.

lead it.

you
were a wildfire.

letting you burn me down
to ashes

was the only way
to know what love feels like.

how beautiful it is to stay soft
in a world filled
with tragedy.

the verse that begins
from
the twist of your mind

and carries me in the midst
of my being
that is what i cannot write.

you lost your
language
under the weight
of their words and you wonder

why
you cannot respond

to the voice
of your own body.

_____

urban slavery.

tread gently
over me.

i am a
homeland
not a battlefield.

it is brutal
to watch you rebuild
yourself
only to let them
in
again.

———————

loop. break it before it breaks you.

how can i not
fall in love
with the way you

create
soft music out of me?

————————

vulnerable.

it can be
a tiring thing

to carry the ruins that lay heavy
on your chest.

to long for a home
a heart
that was never really there.

_____

mirage.

do not close your eyes.
the sun is
rising
in your bones.

you are left
in my breath like
embers
of a dying fire.

maybe it is time
i warm my heart myself.

perhaps it will
make sense

when we learn
to unlearn

the things holding us
back.

there is something magical
about the way
you keep your sorrows

on your lips
and break them into a smile.

_____

strength comes in different smiles.

i am tired of melting
my parts
to light up the darkness

that
flows
through your limbs.

feel
what is falling off
your chest
and
the silence in between.

this is how your heart makes
room for you.

_____

process.

if you are
brave enough to destruct
yourself

you are brave enough
to begin again.

irretrievably
slipping into my skin.
there is cold

and then there is
you.

_____

pores.

to be the most beautiful form
of poetry
let yourself be consumed
by words.

let your every limb
every nerve
every bone and every vein

undulate
to the sound of change

of your skin
into infinite verses.

for only then
you will witness

how amidst the deafening chaos of
this mad world

a poem takes birth.

———————

metamorphosis.

i wake up to you
in the middle of these words

and you keep me
from drifting away.

give yourself
time to
undo the wars

raging inside you.

don't shy away from your
body so soon.

the dawn
is yet to come.
the road is yet to turn.

the wind is yet to
ruffle
through your hair.

the streets
are yet to turn gold
under the sun.

and i
am yet to plant
seeds
on your tired tongue.

———————

bloom before the sun sets.

shutting out the wars
in my head
tonight i choose to curl up
in
your
fleeting
memories.

v i n a t i

let us learn
to love our every detail
before

we let the world
in.

_____

repeat to yourself till your heart
expands with nothing but warm light.

fade into the stars tonight.
the moon is here
to stay.

i soak up
a little more light

every time you make a slit
in my skin.

—————

in our own little ways, we all heal.

do you
see
how my limbs
s p r e a d

when the night
slips
back into me?

this is how i fall
in love.

_____

homecoming.

do not mull over the stories
that you
leave
incomplete.

you are here to follow
the one
that leads you to yourself.

let it melt in you.
the hurt

that is beating rigorously
against your heart.

you were born
a festival.

why miss a chance
to celebrate
yourself?

the moon bends
unevenly

at the corner of my lips
whenever

i like a ritual
breathe your name.

beneath every bruise
there is
a story to tell
and
a world to inspire.

_____

look closely.

these fingers
have gone weak

since the time
i stopped
feeding you verses.

and i'm often asked
why my hands tremble
when
i
write.

listen to me.
you flourish like
the earth
in every void
in every space.

why do you still weep?

_____

remember what you are made of.

it is addictive
to burn
wildly like the sun

when the night falls
all over me.

feed light to your heart.
let it split and spill

the cold
it has been carrying.

let it do what it does best.

let it love.

i have held onto
you
for too long to remember

which parts
do not belong
to me
anymore.

bow down
to the fire in you.

there are too many stories
waiting

beyond this chaos
to taste life.

pull the drawstring and let go.
_____

now.

be with me for a while.
let me learn the art

of carving
people into poetry.

we soak each other
in tales.
half spoken. half bled.

————————

how broken people love.

steal some gentleness
from the sky.

look how it opens
itself
to those willing to drift.

traces of your breath
are gushing
mutely
in my palms.

maybe this is why
i am
more you tonight
than i ever was.

how often
do you let out the screams
that you have been eating?
not biting not chewing

just gulping
and pushing them straight down
to your belly
days after days
seasons after seasons.

tell me. how do you carry
the weight of those
voices
that you have lost

in between the nods
and the smiles
the head bowed
down
the eyes tightly shut

the ears filled with noise
and the skin
marked with dents?

contd.

tell me.
you woman made of the sun.
how do you shrink

within the tiny claws of the
moon?

_____

*war that is brutally quiet within those
walls.*

keep the love wild.

the madness strong.

and the heart tender.

_____

to do list

you would know
why sometimes
things
don't end
on the finish line

when you feel
my presence drifting
back

in your mouth
and
your words begin to break.

even the oceans are
cursed
by those
who cannot swim.

what makes you
think
the mad world would
spare you?

put down your shield darling.
that little
wrecked part of
you
also needs light.

the last breath of the night
lingers along

the edge
of my bed
and we both laze.

a little tired

and a lot in love.

———————

shh.

your mind speaks
and i fail to hold myself
in me.

this is how
you make me lush.

if you have to
prune
your verses to fit within
the edge

of their tongue
you are betraying yourself.

_____

shame.

we eat our grief
with devotion.

fold our breaths.
tie them in
knots

and learn
to breathe with our mouths
hungry for love.

———————

solitude.

the hardest part
of letting you go
is
learning

to fall back on my spine
which is too weak

to carry
the weight of
our past.

to feel the wild
in
your blood
and let it slip away.
it is a dangerous thing.

it often kills
without a trace.

stop seeking solace
in the
falling rain

when darling you are
meant to rise.

there are poems
seeping through the crevices
you left behind.

gentle on the eyes.
rough on the tongue.

so deeply rooted in me
yet clawing their way to the paper.

i am learning
how not to split open the

sky

every time the moon
calls out my name.

_____

moon child.

take care
of the fragile you.

it holds the calm
you are looking for.

all this while
words kept rolling out
of my flesh

to find
a home that fits.

———————

in you.

ABOUT THE AUTHOR

Vinati Bhola is an internationally published poet based in Delhi, India. She works as a lawyer but falls back on poetry time and again to keep up with the monotony of everyday life. Writing since the age of thirteen, she believes poetry is so much more than romanticizing emotions. *"It is an art, as simple as breathing and as complex as living."*

Her first collection of poems *Udaari* is an unbridled downpour of love, madness, chaos and calm that gradually sweeps in at the end. The word *Udaari* has been taken graciously from her native language Punjabi. It means to fly, to spread the wings and take a leap, a quiet soar against the wind.

You can find her presence at
www.writingsofvinati.com
www.instagram.com/writingsofvinati
www.facebook.com/writingsofvinati

30140798R00102

Made in the USA
Middletown, DE
23 December 2018